PRESENTS

THE ULTIMATE GUIDE TO
TIKTOK
2024 EDITION

LittleBrother
BOOKS

Published 2023 Little Brother Books Ltd, Ground Floor,
23 Southernhay East, Exeter, Devon, EX1 1QL
Printed in China. EU address Korte Leemstraat 3,
2018 Antwerpen , Belgium

books@littlebrotherbooks.co.uk | www.littlebrotherbooks.co.uk

The Little Brother Books trademark, email and website addresses and
the IYKYK logo and imprint are sole and exclusive properties of
Little Brother Books Limited.

PARENTAL ADVISORY RECOMMENDED

DIVE INTO TIKTOK!

Since its launch in 2014, TikTok has grown into one of the world's most popular platforms. Here's your totally TikTok rundown…

The stats

Over 3 billion app downloads.

Over 1 billion users worldwide.

Used in 155 different countries.

Most users are under 20 years old.

Over 1 billion video views each day.

A brief history of TikTok...

Back in 2014, a little app called Musical.ly was launched. The idea was simple: users could upload short lip-syncing videos. In 2017, Musical.ly joined forces with Chinese app Douyin to create TikTok! In 2018, TikTok was passing Facebook and Instagram in the daily downloads charts. During the global pandemic in 2020, TikTok became a place for everyone, including celebrities, to have fun, laugh and be creative. In 2024 TikTok is one of the most-popular apps on the planet!

It's funny

You won't be scrolling TikTok for long before something makes you laugh. Reading a pet's thoughts, being part of a prank or watching someone tell jokes – it's guaranteed to give you the giggles.

It's inspiring

Whether it's an art tutorial, a room transformation or a make-up vid, TikTok gives us ideas!

We love TikTok because...

It's a window to the world

It doesn't matter if you are a blockbusting movie star or a supermarket cashier – TikTok is open to everyone. In a few scrolls you can travel continents, peek into celebrity homes and all from the comfort of your own home.

It's current

How many new trends have you discovered through TikTok? What about new music or artists you may not have heard of before? TikTok is one of the best ways to keep your finger on the pulse!

Safe and sound

Feeling safe while you scroll, and create, videos is very important. Here's a rundown of what you need to know about staying safe on TikTok.

Restricted Mode

If you are worried about seeing something you'd rather not, you can **view TikTok in restricted mode**. This will **filter out** any videos that might be inappropriate or upsetting. All you have to do is head to your settings, then **digital wellbeing**.

Privacy matters

If you want to use TikTok just to watch videos, or if you're not quite ready to share your vids with the world, make sure your **account is private**. You can do this in the 'privacy' section of your settings.

Screentime

It can be easy to **lose time on TikTok**. Watching your favourite creator or following a new trend. But too much time on a tiny screen isn't great for your mental health, as well as your eyesight! **Toggle the screentime button on**, in the digital wellbeing section of your settings.

You are not alone

If you do **feel unsafe**, or **unhappy on TikTok**, there are things you can do. TikTok has a **reporting function** for videos and accounts that are not abiding by the rules. Just hit the share button and find the **warning triangle**.

Take a break!

TikTok has been around for nearly ten years and it's not going anywhere soon. So, if you find yourself looking at your app for a long time, or obsessing over your video views – **step away for a while**. You'll like it even more when you get back on it.

No one, friends or everyone?

There are a whole lot of options you can play with in the privacy part of your settings. You can decide if your **avatar can be found**, if you want anyone to duet with your videos, if anyone can **comment on your videos** and who is **allowed to message you**. Chat through these options with a grown-up if you're not sure what to do.

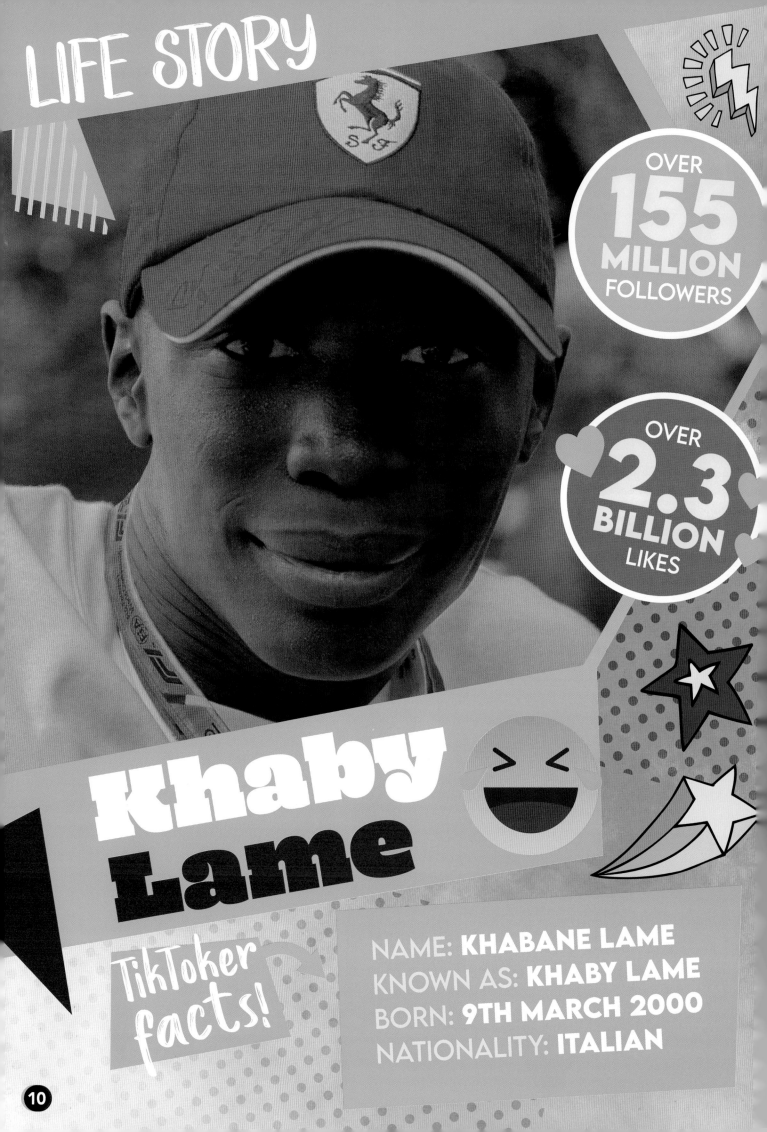

OVER
155
MILLION
FOLLOWERS

OVER
2.3
BILLION
LIKES

khaby Lame

TikToker facts!

NAME: **KHABANE LAME**
KNOWN AS: **KHABY LAME**
BORN: **9TH MARCH 2000**
NATIONALITY: **ITALIAN**

WHERE IT ALL BEGAN...

Khaby was made redundant from his job when the global pandemic hit in 2020. While he waited to see what he could do next, Khaby started making TikTok videos and soon gained followers.

HOW HE SHOT TO FAME

His first TikToks were pretty simple. They involved Khaby either dancing or watching video games. However, it was when Khaby discovered the 'duet' function that he really came into his own. Khaby stitched together life hack videos with a video of himself doing the same thing far simpler. His trademark look of disbelief and hand gesture became an instant hit.

WHERE IS HE NOW?

Quite simply, at the top. With 155.8 million followers and 2.3 billion likes, he's constantly vying for the position of most-loved TicToker on the planet. He's collaborated with McDonalds, Netflix, Hugo Boss and Juventus and even got invited to the 2023 Oscars!

MOST WATCHED VIDEO

Despite the amazing collabs and celebrity lifestyle, Khaby's most popular video is a classic. It starts with a video of a passenger adding an extra wing mirror to their car so that they don't open the door into traffic. Khaby wordlessly explains, in his usual manner, that the same effect can be achieved by opening the car window!

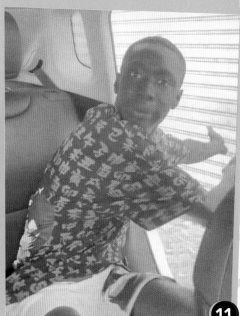

Trends Taking Over

A year is a long time in TikTok land. Take a look at what's exploded over our timelines in 2023!

The Wednesday Dance

Wednesday became one of Netflix's most-watched shows in 2023, making its lead character, Jenny Ortega, an instant star. However, it was episode four's iconic dance scene that has inspired this latest TikTok craze. Wednesday busted her unique moves on the dancefloor to The Cramps' 1981 song 'Goo Goo Muck', inspiring thousands of homages.

♪ TikTok
heyitsbessma

Autonomous Sensory Meridian Response is basically a very long-winded way of saying: Something that gives you goosebumps when you hear it. These videos have exploded over TikTok this year and range from cooking videos, refilling fridges, unboxing and whispering. Creators use a special, supersonic mic to pick up and magnify even the smallest of sounds.

13

Expression challenge

Get your acting skills kicked into gear with this funny challenge, using 'Why You Asking All Them Questions?' from Spoken Reasons. The audio snippit poses several questions that users have been matching to their own, their pet's and even their baby's expressions. Ciara's version has had almost 500k likes alone.

Try not to dance or sing challenge - 90's Edition

Try not to react

TikTok is all about music and dancing, right? Well, this trend challenges users to fight all those instincts! Using a megamix of different songs, creators try their best to stay as still as possible. Sounds easy? Just think how you feel when your favourite song appears out of no where. You've got to move! These videos are particularly hard for dancers like Marco Andre Da Silva.

Get ready with me

These videos are so good, because they often show the reality of what it takes for TicTokers to look good! They can show aspirational morning routines to getting ready for work or a night out. Some are quite basic, such as grabbing a piece of toast while packing a bag, to a full morning routine of workouts, smoothies and journaling. They are fun glimpses into other people's lives, which is why they have become so popular! This vid from Kylie Jenner has over 12 million likes!

TikTok
@kyliejenner

Nick Cage vs Pedro Pascal

TikTok
@silvurlinings

Thanks to the *Mandelorian* and *The Last of Us*, Pedro Pascal has been all over TikTok, and none more so than in this funny meme-turned-video. The premise is simple. Nick Cage is angry, Pedro Pascal is joyous – you get to decide what situation these two characters fit into!

LIFE STORY

OVER
81
MILLION
FOLLOWERS

OVER
768
MILLION
LIKES

Mr Beast

TikToker facts!

NAME: **JIMMY DONALDSON**
KNOWN AS: **MR BEAST**
BORN: **7TH MAY 1998**
NATIONALITY: **AMERICAN**

WHERE IT ALL BEGAN...

Mr Beast, AKA Jimmy, started posting when he was just 13 years old. Just like Khaby Lame, his first videos were gaming and reaction videos, but Jimmy's personality meant that he quickly started to get followers. He changed his style when his popularity grew, and he began to make challenge videos and videos where he helped people.

The World's Largest Minion

▷ 16M

HOW HE SHOT TO FAME

The video that shot Mr Beast into social media big leagues was a challenge video uploaded to YouTube that saw Jimmy counting to 100,000. By the end of 2018, he had also given out $1million in stunts.

WHERE IS HE NOW?

Mr Beast is now one of the top five TicTokers on the planet. He collaborates with brands and production companies to produce a mix of charity giveaways (like tipping a waitress with a new car) and crazy stunts, such as being buried alive.

MOST WATCHED VIDEO

Mr Beast is famous for his incredible generosity, and this video is no exception. In this stunt, Jimmy's friend, Jimmy Darts, asked shoppers if they follow Mr Beast on TikTok. When they say yes, and confirm it on the app, they are in for a BIG surprise. The first lady Jimmy finds is taken outside with her son (who reassures his mum that everything is going to be OK as he knows Karate!) and she is given a brand new car by Mr Beast himself! Lesson learned. If anyone asks you if you follow Mr Beast – always say yes!

yes to

brand

I cannot

TikTok Spot

These are some of the most-watched videos on TikTok, but can you spot the three differences we have made in each one?

Colour in a heart when you spot each difference.

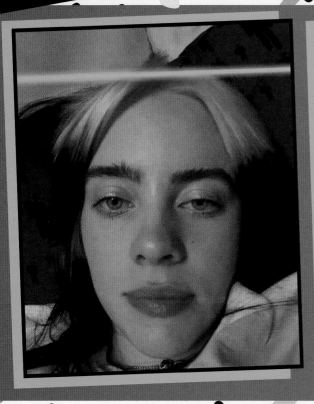

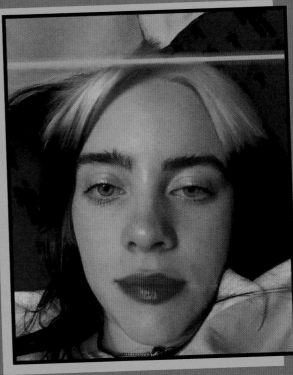

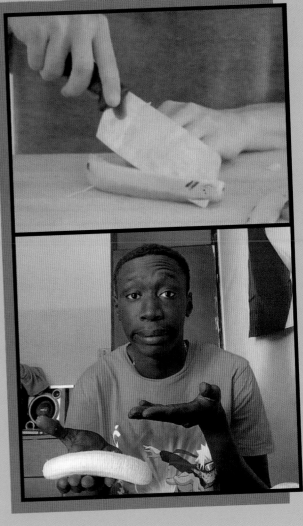

ANSWERS ON p76!

Making Tracks

Sometimes it's hard to tell if a song becomes famous because of TikTok or is on TikTok because it's famous! Here's a run-down of the tracks currently filling up our timelines.

The King Khan & BBQ Show - Love You So

The opening few seconds of this track will be instantly recognisable to any TikTok user. **The song has been played over 1 billion times** with the track being used for everything from **life hacks** to **dance videos**.

Miley Cyrus - Flowers

When Miley released her ultimate payback song after breaking up with husband Liam Hemsworth, the internet (and TikTok) totally got on board. **From analysing the lyrics and video**, to creating **tributes** and **standalone dances**. One of the most colourful, and most liked, versions is @Kelli's dance video.

TikTok @happykelli

Tik @hap

Sam Smith & Kim Petras - Unholy

This **epic tune** has been used to **add drama to videos** – and it certainly works! It has been used on everything from **recipes to room transformations and makeovers**. It's also a favourite for travellers who like to add drama to spectacular scenery.

Meghan Trainor - Made You Look

The song that spawned a **brand-new dance trend**, 'Made you Look' has been used thousands of times thanks to its simple steps and catchy theme. This video with Meghan and actor Penn Badgley has racked up **18,000 likes** to date!

Taylor Swift - Antihero

This track has **blown up on TikTok** thanks to its **honest, fun lyrics and amazing video**. The chorus has been used for countless memes, while other accounts love to deep dive into the meaning behind the words and imagery used. **Take a listen and see what you think!**

LIFE STORY

OVER **50** MILLION FOLLOWERS

OVER **150** MILLION FOLLOWERS

Charli D'Amilio & Dixie D'Amelio

TikToker facts!

KNOWN AS: **CHARLI AND DIXIE**
BORN: **1ST MAY 2004 & 12TH AUGUST 2001**
NATIONALITY: **AMERICAN**

WHERE IT ALL BEGAN...

Charli started posting to TikTok in 2019 with a short lip sync video, but she quickly started gaining followers and now switches places with Khaby Lame for the title of Most Loved TicToker. Dixie followed in her sister's footsteps a few years later and is now almost as popular as her little sis.

HOW THEY SHOT TO FAME

The truth is, neither of the D'Amelio sisters know quite why they have become so popular on TikTok and around the world. They simply jumped on the TikTok train at the right time and know what their followers want. By keeping up with trends, and setting them, too!

WHERE ARE THEY NOW?

Still some of the most popular ladies on the internet, the D'Amelio siblings have had their own TV shows and countless collaborations. Dixie is releasing new music while Charli has turned her hand to presenting at the Nickelodeon Kids' Choice Awards.

MOST WATCHED VIDEOS

Charli's most watched video is super simple. She is being driven to or from an event, wearing a hoody with a fresh face and no make-up. The whole video sees Charli trying out a new audio trend. It proves that Charli's fans love her for her realness, rather than anything fake or filtered. WARNING: Explicit language.

Similarly, Dixie's video is also shot in the back of a car, showing off her incredible cropped pixie cut. You can tell Dixie is loving her new look, as are her fans as this video has been liked over 3 million times!

THE CROSSWORD craze

How well do you know your favourite app?
Solve the clues to complete the grid!

Down

1. To do something really well.

2. Hearts.

4. Watch this tally shoot up when a video goes viral.

6. The term used when something or someone has had a makeover (4, 2)

7. Gossip.

10. Finished your video, now it's time to _ _ _ _ it.

Across

1. The name given or hashtag added to a video where someone tells a tale or experience.

3. The words that mean something is kinda under the radar (3, 3).

5. Four crossed lines that can be used before a word to search something or to tag your video.

8. The name for all the people who like your account.

9. The three letters that mean 'profile picture'.

11. Another name for a piece of music.

ANSWERS ON p76!

TOTALLY TRIPPY TIKTOK!

These videos will have you questioning if magic is real, or are these creators just masters of the video edit?

Optical illusions

Sometimes, the things we see can get muddled up in our brains. TicToker Sabrina Reacts loves an optical illusion. In the video below she shows us how, if we turn this image of a flight of stairs upside down, the stairs are also upside down – until we blink that is!

Face-paint freakout

Mimi Choi's makeup is so realistic you'll be questioning your own eyes, and maybe a few of Mimi's eyes too! Her account is definitely worth checking out if you like mind-bending make-up illusions. You'll be amazed what this TikTokker can do with some face-paint and a crazy imagination.

Training day

Zach King is the undisputed, well, King of the TikTok illusion. His edits are so smooth you'll believe he really can turn a watering can into a football strip, and a football into a dalmatian! Zach's been around for a few years now, but his videos are just as addictive as ever. Clear your schedule if you want to take a look at his feed!

Flipped lids

Pete Firman is an old-school magician on an ultra-modern platform. His videos are quick, fun and will leave you desperate to find out his secrets. Check out the still from this video, the lids of the two boxes are the same size! Don't believe us? Check out Pete's account to discover how!

LIFE STORY

OVER **88** MILLION FOLLOWERS

OVER **768** MILLION LIKES

Addison Rae

TikToker facts!

NAME: **ADDISON RAE EASTERLING**
KNOWN AS: **ADDISON RAE**
BORN: **6TH OCTOBER 2000**
NATIONALITY: **AMERICAN**

WHERE IT ALL BEGAN...

In 2019 Addison was babysitting when she decided to post a video on TikTok just for fun. That video got so many likes, Addison became an almost overnight sensation. A few months after joining TikTok she teamed up with the Hype House collaboration and her entry into TikTok stardom was complete.

WHERE IS SHE NOW?

With over 88 million followers, Addison is always one of the top 5 TicTokers on the planet. Addison's not stopping there, though. She's also released her own music, got her own fashion and beauty range, and had collaborations with Versace, Nintendo and Pandora – to name a few!

MOST WATCHED VIDEO

This simple video of Addison trying out a lipgloss one-handed in the back of a car might look like your average Addison vid, but it has leapt to the top of her most-watched list thanks to a comment from *Stranger Things* superstar, Joseph Quinn!

celebrity TAKEOVER

Some stars become famous because of TikTok, but these guys were already stratospheric before joining the app! Check out the most-popular celebrity accounts.

Will Smith

Will Smith has topped the celebrity TikTok leagues for a few years now thanks to his superstar status and commitment to fun, highly edited videos. Will's 73+ million followers are taken with him as he travels the globe, hangs out at home and reacts to other viral videos on the internet.

FOLLOWERS: **73 MILLION+**
MOST WATCHED VIDEO: **MEN IN BLACK MIRROR WIPE 271+ MILLION LIKES**
MY FAVOURITE WILL SMITH VIDEO:

Billie Eilish

Not many people can match Billie's coolness quota, and her fans have made sure that the singer and style icon is a TikTok superstar, too. With videos that range from song snippets to messing about with her friends, Billie is always real and never too polished – which is why so many people love her!

FOLLOWERS: **47 MILLION+**
MOST WATCHED VIDEO: **TIME WARP VIDEO 40+ MILLION LIKES**
MY FAVOURITE BILLIE VIDEO:

The Tortilla Challenge

The Rock

One of the nicest guys in show business has to have an awesome TikTok account, right? Absolutely. The Rock's mix of glamour (getting ready for the Oscars) and home life (letting is daughters cover him in pink face paint) make his account an irresistible follow.

FOLLOWERS: **69.6 MILLION**
MOST WATCHED VIDEO: **TORTILLA CHALLENGE WITH KEVIN HART 24.1 MILLION VIEWS**
WARNING: EXPLICIT LANGUAGE

MY FAVOURITE ROCK VIDEO:

Selena Gomez

One of the things fans love about Selena is her love of posting glam shots, mixed with reality. Selena has been vocal about body positivity and self-esteem, and she shows this in the content she puts out on her feed. As well as showcasing her Rare Beauty range, she posts behind the scenes videos and games with friends.

FOLLOWERS: **57.8 MILLION**
MOST WATCHED VIDEO: **GETTING READY FOR A 6AM FLIGHT 206.9 MILLION VIEWS**

MY FAVOURITE SELENA VIDEO:

Jason Derulo

Another celebrity who always finds his way into the top TikTok celebrities list is musician, Jason. Despite being known for his music, Jason has also embraced TikTok with his stunts, duets and trends. We reckon if Jason had not already made it big as a musician, he'd be giving Mr Beast a run for his money!

FOLLOWERS: **57.7 MILLION**

MOST WATCHED VIDEO: **DANCING WITH @NOELGOESCRAZY 44.5 MILLION VIEWS**

MY FAVOURITE JASON VIDEO:

Kylie Jenner

No run down of the internet's most-popular celebrities would be complete without one of the Kardashian / Jenner family. Kylie takes top spot as the TikTok family member with the most followers thanks to her mix of getting-ready videos, family cameos and general slaying glamour. We also love the cuteness when Stormi and baby Aire make an appearance.

FOLLOWERS: **52.3 MILLION**

MOST WATCHED VIDEO: **DANCING WITH KHLOE KARDASHIAN 120.4MILLION VIEWS**

MY FAVOURITE KYLIE VIDEO:

JoJo Siwa

JoJo is about so much more than bows. She's still got that high energy and colourful vibe, but these days you'll find her dancing, having fun, making her followers laugh and being as positive and inspirational as she can. JoJo's energy and optimism is infectious!

FOLLOWERS: **45.9 MILLION**
MOST WATCHED VIDEO: **DANCING INTO THE SEA WITH MICKEY! 68.6 MILLION VIEWS**
MY FAVOURITE JOJO VIDEO:

BTS

The fact that BTS are so high up in the celebrity TikTok charts could be considered cheating – there are seven of them after all! However, their account just keeps on growing thanks to their dedicated fans, and the band's dedication to the dance video! Everyone has a favourite BTS member, and luckily the band are great at taking it turns to share the TikTok limelight.

FOLLOWERS: **58.8 MILLION**
MOST WATCHED VIDEO: **DANCING TO DYNAMITE 151.1 MILLION VIEWS**
MY FAVOURITE BTS VIDEO:

OVER 92 MILLION FOLLOWERS

OVER 2.3 BILLION LIKES

Bella Poarch

TikToker facts!

NAME: **DENARIE TAYLOR**
KNOWN AS: **BELLA POARCH**
BORN: **7TH FEBRUARY 1998**
NATIONALITY: **AMERICAN / PILIPINO**

WHERE IT ALL BEGAN...

Like many of our most-famous TikTok stars, Bella's roots are in gaming. Her first videos were mostly about cosplay and video games, and it wasn't until she posted her infamous 'Soph Aspin Send' by Millie B lip-sync video that she catapulted into the big leagues. And we mean BIG. That particular video became the most-watched TikTok of all time and continues to keep its spot in the most-watched lists.

WHERE IS SHE NOW?

Although Bella is still big on TikTok, it's her music career that is really on the rise. She's teamed up with musician and bestie Grimes and has released an album entitled *Dolls*. You can still catch her every day on the app, showing you what she's been up to, dancing and creating outfits in her own unique style.

MOST WATCHED VIDEO

Do we even need to say? Bella's iconic, head-bopping video is still her number one liked and viewed video of all time.

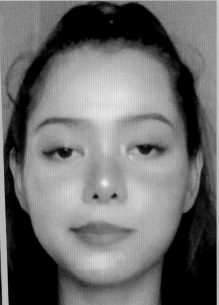

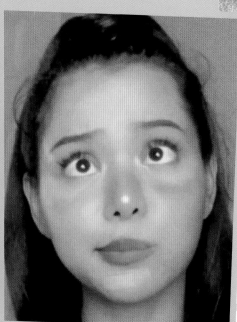

A DAY IN THE TIKTOK LIFE

Let these TicTokers walk you through a typical day in the life of a content creator.

8am

BREAKFAST TIME WITH JOSH ELKIN

Breakfast is more than just a piece of toast as you rush out the door, if you are a content creator — breakfast is an event. From elaborate smoothies to bowls of perfectly balanced bircher muesli. Of course, for TikTok chef, Josh Elkin, his breakfast potato recipe has been liked almost 3 million times. Now that is a popular breakfast!

10am

GET READY WITH CHARLI

Whether it's a full face of make-up, or a quick moisturise and spritz of dry shampoo, influencers can't help but share how they get ready in the morning. This quick video by TikTok Queen, Charli, shows how she keeps it simple for a morning workout.

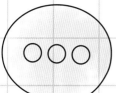

12pm

WALK WITH ABBY

You've got to get in that daily dose of vitamin D – especially if the rest of the time you are in a dark room, sitting on your bum editing videos! This video with Abby Roberts and friends takes you all around her favourite vintage shops on sunny Brick Lane in London.

♪ TikTok
@abbyroberts

Thrifting in London Brick Lane

1pm — LUNCH WITH ADDISON

If you haven't taken a video of your lunch, did you even eat it? Addison's video of her delicious pasta dinner (with a bit of help from Moana's Gramma Tala) has been liked over a million times. Addison looks genuinely delighted with her Italian feast!

3pm

FILMING CONTENT WITH MR BEAST

The life of a TicToker is non-stop, so the afternoon lull is a pretty good time to record a video, ready to post when you are rushed off your feet. A quick lip-sync, outfit change or, if you are Mr Beast, tipping a waitress with a car! It's all in a day's work for the app's most-generous content creator.

you to cry

TikTok
@mrbeast

5pm

GETTING READY WITH BELLA

When you have millions of followers and a hoard of famous friends, your diary is bound to be packed with events, parties and launches. As well as the event itself, influencers love to document the getting ready process — and we love seeing it! Bella Poarch's team are on hand to make sure the TicToker-turned-musician always looks on point.

TikTok
@bellapoarch

7pm

PARTY TIME WITH KHABY

TicTokers love to give their followers a glimpse behind the red-velvet rope of VIP areas in their videos. Ice sculptures, goody bags, celebrities and lots and LOTS of selfies. Khaby Lame was so stoked to get an invitation to the Oscars that he made this sweet rags-to-riches video charting his journey to the red carpet.

♪ **TikTok**
@khaby.lame

11pm BEDTIME WITH BILLIE

OK, so maybe not ALL influencers will be in bed by 11pm, but lots of them will be – knowing they have another full day of creating content for their millions of followers. Billie looks so comfortable in this video, we just want to grab our favourite oversized hoodie and jump on the sofa next to her!

OVER **76** MILLION FOLLOWERS

OVER **1** BILLION LIKES

Zach King

TikToker facts!

NAME: **ZACHARY KING**
KNOWN AS: **ZACH KING**
BORN: **4TH FEBRUARY 1990**
NATIONALITY: **AMERICAN**

WHERE IT ALL BEGAN...

Zach started his content life in 2011 on YouTube with a video that mashed up two of the internet's favourite things: cats and Star Wars. His Jedi battling kittens video saw his popularity rise, and in 2013 he was named as one of YouTube's 25 most promising young film-makers in America. Back when TikTolk was known as Musical.ly, Zach posted a video that saw him seemingly escape from a prison cell.

WHERE IS HE NOW?

Thanks to another huge franchise (this time Harry Potter) Zach created one of the most-watched videos on TikTok. He now makes videos that are so complex, mindboggling, and flawless that he is still one of the top TicTokers in the world and has partnered up with the biggest brands on the planet, including Disney, Nike, Apple and Coca-Cola.

MOST WATCHED VIDEO

With over 2 billion views, the broomstick fake-out video is still Zach's biggest success. With numbers that high, it's no wonder the brands are falling over themselves to work with TikTok's biggest and best illusionist.

Mental Health MATTERS

Social media can be fun, creative and inspiring, but it can also affect your mental health. Follow these steps to ensure you feel good on and off the app.

Listen to your heart

Our bodies are really smart. They give us **little warnings** when things aren't quite right, sending signals to your brain to do something about it. The same goes when it comes to your mental health. If you find yourself **feeling anxious** when you have posted a video or have been scrolling through your feed – it could mean you need to **take a break.**

Sticks and stones

Have you heard the saying: 'Sticks and stones may break my bones, but words will never hurt me'? Well, it's nonsense. **Words can have an upsetting and lasting effect on your mental health,** especially if you are particularly sensitive to negative comments. A sure-fire way to protect yourself from comments like this is to **close the comments** on any videos you post.

TikTok uncensored

As much as the app tries to monitor the content that is uploaded, damaging and upsetting videos are posted all the time and can pop up on your screen. If this happens, **ask a grown up to help you** with the **security setting on your app**. Make sure you talk about anything you have seen that is playing on your mind. It is always better to talk, than to bottle something up.

Filter your triggers

Social media can make you feel **'triggered'**. Feeling triggered simply means that when you see a certain image, person or theme, it makes you **feel sad or uncomfortable**. For some, a trigger can be seeing expensive clothes you can't afford, **heavily filtered pictures of impossible beauty standards**, or even innocent pictures, such as a puppy if your dog has just passed away. The best way to sort this out is to **unfollow** any accounts that make you feel a certain way, or click the share arrow, then click 'not interested'. This way, the TikTok algorithm will start to learn what you do and don't want to see.

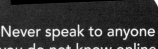

Remember

Never speak to anyone you do not know online and talk to a grown-up if you see or read anything upsetting.

Rise to the TOP

These videos have been creeping up the list of most watched videos this year. Keep an eye on those view counters as they could be on their way to becoming the most-watched of all time!

1.1 BILLION VIEWS

ZACH KING: HIDE AND SEEK 1.1 BILLION

An oldie, but still a goodie. This one just keeps hanging around the most-watched charts and was still just as big in 2023. Zach's use of optical illusion, seamless editing and simple ideas make him just so watchable!

398 MILLION VIEWS

DAEXO BABY 398 MILLION VIEWS

Everyone loves a cute baby. Just LOOK at those cheeks! But add to that a winning smile and a trend-worth soundtrack, it's no wonder this video is racking up the views year on year.

390 MILLION VIEWS

390 MILLION VIEWS

KOOL KID KELLY: HOW DID SHE KNOW THIS DANCE? 390 MILLION VIEWS

Prank turned dance video, this TikTok has the comments section divided. At first, Kool Kid pretends to trip down the escalator, causing concern to the two girls behind him – he then breaks out into a well-known TikTok dance, only to have one of the girls join in! The question is, is the second dancer in on the joke or did she just join in for fun?

JORDI KOALITIC: SAIL! 390 MILLION VIEWS

Jordi takes us behind the scenes of some beautiful photography in this short TikTok, revealing how string and a few simple props can create stunning effects. You also need a really good camera and editing software, but that bit doesn't make it in the vid!

318 MILLION VIEWS

303 MILLION VIEWS

NADIR SAILOV: A FROG CLIMBED INTO THE CLOSET 318 MILLION VIEWS

We all love a prank video, but in this TikTok, it's the viewer who gets pranked. Warning: Spoilers ahead! Don't be fooled by the title of this video, there is no frog. As the viewer patiently waits for the drawer to be opened and a little frog to come out, they are suddenly faced with a spider animation crawling out of the drawer and jumping towards the screen. Terrifying!

KHABY LAME: COULD BE THE NEW KHABY 303 MILLION VIEWS

Again, another classic that is keeping up with all the newbies on the block. This is one of the videos that made Khaby a TikTok legend. It starts with a video of a girl seemingly getting her pigtails stuck in a car window and then cut off, with no way to stop it. Khaby explains, in his usual fashion, that she simply could have wound down the window to free herself!

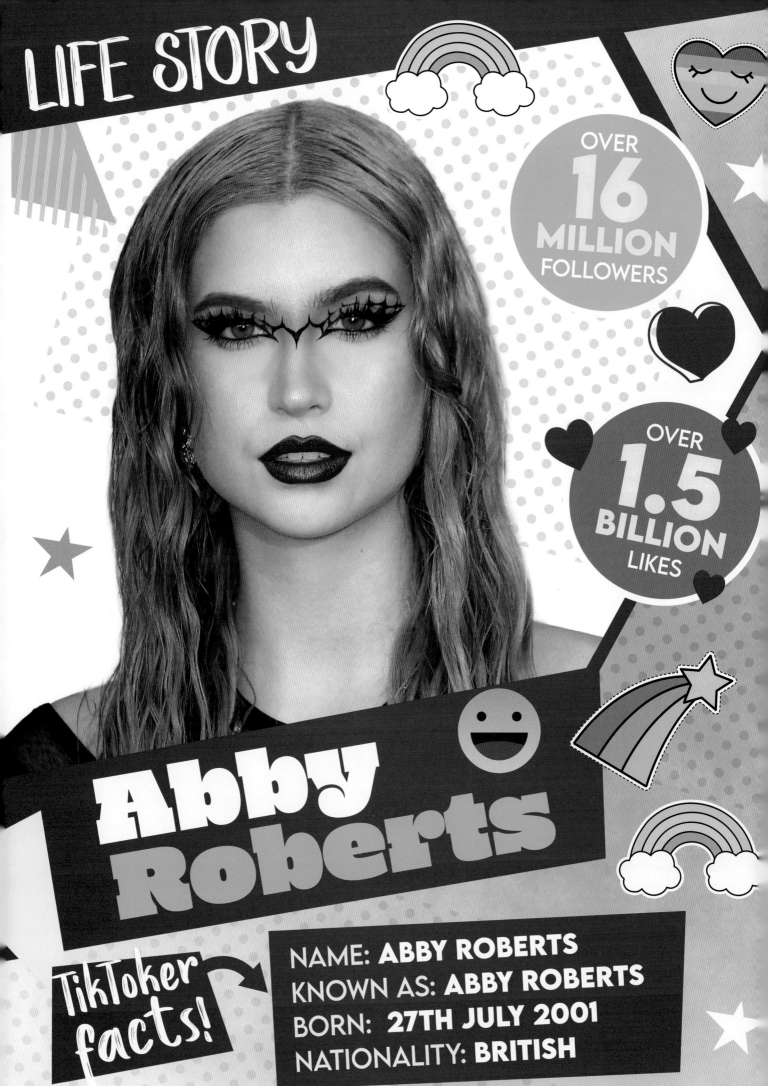

OVER **16** MILLION FOLLOWERS

OVER **1.5** BILLION LIKES

Abby Roberts

TikToker facts!

NAME: **ABBY ROBERTS**
KNOWN AS: **ABBY ROBERTS**
BORN: **27TH JULY 2001**
NATIONALITY: **BRITISH**

WHERE IT ALL BEGAN...

Abby began her career as a social media star at the age of 11, posting make-up tutorial videos to YouTube. She gained a following and began uploading to different social media accounts including, of course, TikTok.

WHERE IS SHE NOW?

Abby is one of the most-liked make-up influencers in the UK and has even been a guest on the make-up artist talent show, *Glow Up*. On TikTok, she is known for her make-up transformations, quirky make-up looks and fashion hauls, as well as videos that give us a glimpse into her world.

MOST WATCHED VIDEO

Abby uses a filter to choose the look she is going to create for Halloween. Landing on Frankie Stein from *Monster High*, Abbey shows how she transforms herself using incredible make-up techniques and a pretty snazzy wig.

FEARLESS fashion

These TicToker are making waves in the fashion world from high-end to high street!

@TRENDYCURVY

Kristine loves a fashion hack, and she fills her feed by trying out these hacks IRL. She shows outfits she has put together for events, fashion hauls and tips for dressing if you have a similar body shape. We love Kristine's upbeat account that is full of positivity.

@YOUNGEMPERORS

French couple Isabelle and Nelson are about as far away from an ASOS fashion haul vid as you can possibly be. They create stylised, artistic videos in matching flawless outfits that can be at once beautiful and a little quirky. Their account is strangely addictive!

@KERIFAY
Full of try-on videos and quick hair tutorials, Keri is a no-nonsense fashion influencer with some great ideas. She's simple, inspirational, and you'll love checking out her glamorous NYC flat.

@IAMDANIELSIMMONS
Photographer Daniel knows how to shoot a perfectly lit video, he also knows a thing or two about style. His feed is mostly filled with GRWM videos, shot on the same background, with a similar format each time. It's super fashionable, super cool, and super watchable.

@WISDM8
Model Wisdom loves to take his TikTok followers behind the scenes on photoshoots, unboxing gifted fashion with him, and creating some wild and wacky videos. Wisdom makes the intimidating world of fashion, fun!

Top 10 Fashion Brands on TikTok

1. @LouisVuitton
2. @Zara
3. @Shien_official
4. @Gymshark
5. @Adidas
6. @Nike
7. @Dior
8. @Balenciaga
9. @burberry
10. @Gucci

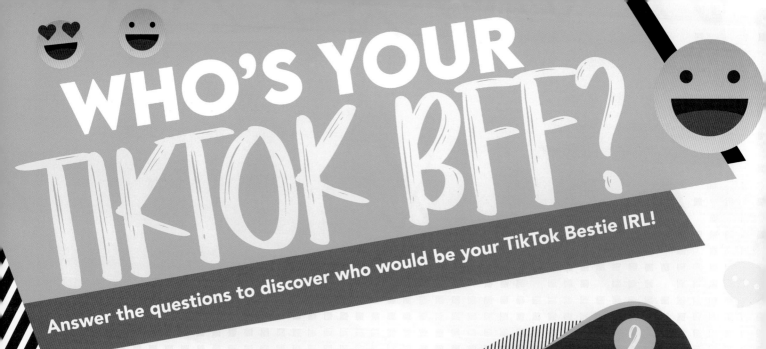

WHO'S YOUR TIKTOK BFF?

Answer the questions to discover who would be your TikTok Bestie IRL!

1

The best videos on TikTok make you:

a Want to watch more videos by that creator

b Surprise you

c Make you smile

2

Your next TikTok video must be about one of these things. Which would you choose?

a Style

b A trending transition or story

c A challenge

3

Which bit of kit would you love to add to your TikTok videos?

a Cool lighting

b Video editing software

c Hidden camera equipment

4

What's your favourite school subject?

a Dance / PE

b Art, design or drama

c Business Studies

5

Which of these would be your ideal get together?

a A party with dancing and music
b Movie night
c Going out for burgers

6

Which of these best describes you?

a Friendly, stylish, cool
b Quirky, creative, fun
c Generous, fearless, silly

Mostly As
CHARLI & DIXIE

Fun, fashion and style – the three things that would make you and the D'Amelio sisters friends for life. A joint GRWM video, nailing the latest dance routine then heading out to a cool launch event – or just chilling with your friends. TikTok for you is all about checking out the latest trends and seeing what your fave influencers are up to.

Mostly Bs
ZACH KING

You and king of illusion Zach would get on like a house on fire, that turns into a candle, that morphs into a kitten. I mean, just your average Zach King video, right? You like things to look as good as they can before hitting the post button, and you like to trick your viewers with your cheeky ideas.

Mostly Cs
MR BEAST

Up for a challenge? Mr Beast (AKA Jimmy) would be right there with you. You both love having fun, pushing yourself, and also being generous to others – so you would be the perfect TikTok besties! After all, TikTok is about having fun, and you two would certainly have that!

LIFE STORY

OVER
15
MILLION
FOLLOWERS

OVER
395
MILLION
LIKES

Holly H

TikToker facts!

NAME: **HOLLY HUBERT**
KNOWN AS: **HOLLY H**
BORN: **17TH OCTOBER 1996**
NATIONALITY: **BRITISH**

WHERE IT ALL BEGAN...

Holly started posting videos on Vine when she was 18, moving on to TikTok way back when it was called Musical.ly. Holly has a talent for make-up, but she's also great at lip-sync and hopping on all the latest dance trends.

WHERE IS SHE NOW?

Holly has used her TikTok and other social media platforms to launch her own podcast, become a radio host and also team up with fashion brand Pretty Little Thing and Disney. She's still posting content to keep her fans happy, too!

MOST WATCHED VIDEO

Counting on your fingers doesn't exactly sound entertaining but, somehow, Holly manages to make a fun and challenging video all at once. A bit of clever video editing and you'll want to see if you can do the same. Check out whistle challenge on TikTok to see more of the same style videos.

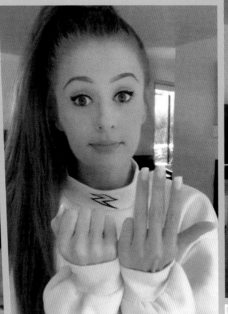

Let's dance!

A big part of TikTok's rise to social media domination is thanks to the dance crazes that have swept the app since its launch. Check out some of the top trending dances and dancers on TikTok right now!

Savage

Although this video by @keke. janajah was posted all the way back in 2020, it's still one of the biggest dances on TikTok thanks to the Megan Thee Stallion soundtrack and incredible moves.

Blinding Lights

Despite first being used in 2020, this is still super-popular thanks to the simple moves and catchy synth-pop music. Extra points for doing the dance with a straight face and getting family members involved!

Calm Down

This one should only be attempted by viral dance pros! Even if you can't quite master the moves, you'll have loads of fun watching the super-sleek dancers in the vids and giving it a go if you feel confident enough.

What's up buster?

One of the newest dances on the block has been attempted, rather successfully, by Brookie and Jessie – the ladies behind last year's Jiggle Jiggle trend. With similar moves and a catchy song – looks like this one is going to get bigger and bigger!

Do it To it

This dance trend has become incredibly popular thanks to its simple choreography and step-by-step moves. Easy to learn, but still makes a super-effective video. There are millions of versions to watch online, too!

Am I ready?

People can't help creating dances as soon as a Lizzo song drops. 'Am I Ready' is no exception! Thankfully this upbeat dance isn't too complicated, you'll just need lots of energy and a big smile to pull it off!

Words on TikTok

Match these scrambled words to their solutions!

ANSWERS ON p76!

1 PLUDOA

2 IVDOE

3 KLISE

4 WIEVS

5 TEDI

6 TGENDNRI

7 ADCEN

8 ATORTILU

9 OSYMTERTI

a VIDEO

b LIKES

c UPLOAD

d TRENDING

e TUTORIAL

f EDIT

g STORYTIME

h VIEWS

i DANCE

TRUE OR FALSE?

For a little app that has only been around for a few years, TikTok has racked up some pretty impressive stats. Can you work out which of these are true, and which are false?

1
TIKTOK HAS HAD OVER 3 BILLION DOWNLOADS.

2
TIKTOK WAS THE MOST-DOWNLOADED APP IN 2022.

3
IT HAS OVER 1 BILLION VIEWS A DAY.

4
IT HAS BEEN VALUED AT $300 BILLION.

5
AN AVERAGE USER SPENDS 2 HOURS A DAY ON THE APP.

ANSWERS ON p76!

LIFE STORY

OVER 52 MILLION FOLLOWERS

OVER 1.4 BILLION LIKES

Michael Le

TikToker facts!

NAME: **MICHAEL LE**

KNOWN AS: **MICHAEL LE / JUSTMAIKO**

BORN: **19TH MARCH 2000**

NATIONALITY: **AMERICAN**

WHERE IT ALL BEGAN...

Michael has always loved to dance. He started posting dance videos and tutorials to YouTube and spread his love to Musical.ly in 2016 before it became known as TikTok. He fast became one of the most-followed accounts on the app thanks to his precision moves and ability to spot and create trends.

WHERE IS HE NOW?

Michael is a TikTok superstar. He has performed at the Nickelodeon Kids Choice Awards and collaborated with some huge brands. He posts on TikTok with his little sister Tiffany (who has 3.4 million followers herself!) as well as his two younger brothers. He also likes to post challenge videos and general catch-ups on his page, as well as a whole load of slick dance vids, of course!

MOST WATCHED VIDEO:

Shakira on an escalator 249.5 million views. One of the videos that made Michael a household name was this video from back in 2020. Michael is seen dancing along to Shakira, 'Hips Don't Lie', as he descends an escalator in a busy shopping centre. At one point in the song, Michael stops dancing and sings, well, shouts, along to the song to the surprise of his fellow shoppers!

CRACKING UP

There is nothing more annoying than cracking your phone screen! Can you still work out who these TikTok celebrities are?

ANSWERS ON p76!

1

2

click the link in

Hello Neighbor 2

NAME KEY:

ABBY ROBERTS   WILL SMITH   TAYLOR SWIFT

MEGHAN TRAINOR   MR BEAST   ADDISON RAE

Best in beauty

The beauty influencers you need to be following right now!

@skincarebyhyram

Rather than creating make-up looks, Hyram makes it his job to tell us how to look after our skin. Although some of the products he uses are a little 'out-there' he also throws in some great tips for keeping your skin healthy, and his videos are always super upbeat.

@AbbyRoberts

As well as teaming up with amazing make-up brands, like Morphe, to create her own range, Abby continues to post on TikTok. She creates her signature dramatic looks, quick make-up tutorials and fashion hauls.

@sydney_art

Sydney is a bold, colourful and creative make-up artist. She loves face paint and even uses things like feathers and paper in her creations. Sydney's addictive account sees her transform herself and her friends, as well as recommending products to use.

@nikkietutorials

Nikkie is a true superstar in the make-up world. She creates flawless make-up looks in a fun and friendly way – and tries out all the crazy make-up trends so you don't have to. She's even had her make-up done by Idris and Sabrina Elba for one of her vids!

@meredithduxbury

More is definitely more for Meredith who loves to completely cover her face in the best make-up out there. She creates sleek fashion looks and her feed is filled with tutorials and GRWM vids. Look out for her lip-sync, tutorial mash-ups, too!

LIFE STORY

OVER
32
MILLION
FOLLOWERS

OVER
1.6
BILLION
LIKES

Kyle Thomas

TikToker facts!

NAME: **KYLE THOMAS**
KNOWN AS: **KYLE THOMAS**
BORN: **19TH SEPTEMBER 2004**
NATIONALITY: **BRITISH**

WHERE IT ALL BEGAN...

Kyle began posting videos to TikTok in 2019 and quickly grew his fanbase by creating lip-sync, dance and food tasting videos. He's also a big fan of the animal world, which obviously upped his follower count!

WHERE IS HE NOW?

Kyle was snapped up by Gleam Futures talent agency and made friends with fellow TikTok stars Holly H and Max and Harvey. His feed is filled with content about his 30 pets (including a pair of meercats and a capybara), trying out new food trends and, yes, he still lip-syncs!

MOST WATCHED VIDEO

Capybaras are pretty cute, so this simple video of Kyle sharing his apple with his capy was bound to hit some big numbers!

FOOD HEAVEN

The best foodie influencers and brands to follow.
WARNING: Do not start scrolling if you're hungry!

INFLUENCER

14 MILLION FOLLOWERS

@BAYASHI.TIKTOK

Bayashi's mainly wordless videos are often filmed on a black background with mega ASMR action and lots of funny expressions from Bayashi himself. As well as recipes, Japanese influencer Bayashi also posts collabs, cooking in miniature and 'this or that' style videos.

INFLUENCER

10.7 MILLION FOLLOWERS

TikTok
@newt

@NEWT

American-Vietnamese Newt began his online career on Twitter, but his real success has been on his TikTok account. Posting videos of traditional recipes, his favourite family meals and just the stuff he finds really yummy. Newt's stories and chats to camera make his personality almost as watchable as the food.

INFLUENCER

5.1 MILLION FOLLOWERS

@FITWAFFLE
UK-based Eloise creates easy-to-follow videos of super-delicious desserts and snacks. She's also created two cookbooks and worked with loads of top magazines. Eloise's quick-fire friendly style has attracted millions of fans all over the world.

INFLUENCER

1.5 MILLION FOLLOWERS

TikTok @tigga_mac

@TIGGA_MAC
Newbie on the block, Tigga is one half of an Aussie-based baking company, creating gorgeous cakes. Tigga's speciality is in creating cakes from popular culture, such as the iconic Friends couch. She's also fab at making illusion cakes. One of her most-famous stunts is to create an item out of cake that you would usually find on a supermarket shelf, popping it alongside the real thing, then strolling into the supermarket to take a bite!

BRAND

1.7 MILLION FOLLOWERS

@THEOREOOFFICIAL
If you thought there was only one way to enjoy an Oreo, think again. Oreos have made their entire feed filled with different ways to enjoy the cookie, as well as turning the iconic biscuit into a character all of its own!

BRAND

2.6 MILLION FOLLOWERS

1. Spicy
2. Cheesy G
3. B 5-L

@TACOBELL
Taco Bell have their own in-house influencers, hopping on trends and creating the most up to date content. This could be why they have one of the biggest food-brand followings in the world!

TikTok
@dunkin

AMERICA RUNS ON DUNKIN'

299 THOUSAND FOLLOWERS

@LITTLEMOONSMOCHI
Little Moons jumped on the TikTok trend for mochi (ice cream wrapped in rice flour dough) and it really paid off. Their TikTok account grew by 700% and the product sold out almost everywhere. Their feed is dedicated to the yumminess of mochi and manages to stay almost as up to date and fresh as the mochi itself!

3.1 MILLION FOLLOWERS

TikTok
@dunkin

633 THOUSAND FOLLOWERS

@DUNKIN 3.1
Dunkin Donuts in the US think they are the friendliest brand on the internet, and they could have a point! Why else would superstars Ben Affleck and Jennifer Lopez film a series of videos for them? Even if you're not a donut fan, their account is a really fun follow.

@DORITOS
Doritos know the power of the influencer. Unlike some of the other top brands, Doritos relies mainly on teaming up with the TikTok universe to create its content, from recipe creators, to fashion designers. For a diverse range of vids, Doritos is worth a follow.

MATCH THE MEANING

TO TELL THE TRUTH.

SOMEONE WHO LIKES YOUR ACCOUNT.

SOMETHING THAT HAS BEEN DONE WELL, OR LOOKS AMAZING.

ANOTHER WORD FOR GOSSIP.

TO FIND SOMETHING INCREDIBLY FUNNY.

FOLLOWER

FIRE

NO CAP

DEAD

PUSHING P

RENT FREE

SLAY

TEA

STAN

STAYING TRUE TO YOURSELF.

DESCRIBES SOMETHING THAT YOU THINK IS REALLY GOOD!

TO WORSHIP SOMETHING OR SOMEONE OBSESSIVELY.

SOMETHING THAT YOU CAN'T GET OUT OF YOUR HEAD.

ANSWERS ON p76!

69

IT'S A DOG'S LIFE

TikTok can't get enough of these pawesome pooches. Get ready for wet snoots all round floofy cuteness.

@Tuckerbudzyn

Tucker and owner 'Linda' have been creating hilarious videos for years, but recently the gorgeous golden retriever has been joined by Tucker's son, Tod. Now it's double the fun, double the drool and double the chimken (that's chicken to you and me).

@Whataboutbunny

Bunny the sheepdog might just be the cleverest dog on TikTok. With the help of a large mat of buttons, Bunny can communicate with her owner – even reminding her when it's time to take medicine. This TikTok might be the closest we get to an IRL Doctor Dolittle!

@huxleythepandapuppy

This teeny Parti Pomeranian shot to fame for jumping inside a pumpkin and looking, well, pretty cute to be fair! Since then, his followers have kept on coming and his owners love showing off their cute pup to the world.

@hammyandolivia

Hammy and Olivia are the most famous corgis outside of Buckingham palace. Their barking inner monologues have been making followers laugh for years, but now the pair are branching out. This year, they released Barkuterie, a cookbook filled with doggy friendly platters to share with their humans!

@dougthepug

If we had to compare Doug to a human TicToker, we're talking D'Amelio levels of fame. He's starred in films, advertisements and music videos, had his own book and calendar. He's even met tons of celebrities from Lewis Capaldi to the cast of *Stranger Things* – and he'll do it all for a belly rub. What's not to love?

YOUR DREAM FEED

Imagine you've just been given the keys to TikTok and can do anything you like to create your dream app! Use this page to note down all your favourites!

My top five accounts

1
2
3
4
5

My favourite tracks

1
2
3

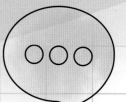

My current fave trend

The top five people I want to follow me

1
2
3
4
5

My fave brands to follow

1
2
3

TikTok TRIVIA

Test your knowledge of your favourite app with these TikTok teasers!

1 WHO IS OLDER, CHARLI OR DIXIE?

2 WHAT DOES IRL STAND FOR?

3 DOES KHABY LAME COME FROM ITALY OR FRANCE?

4 WHAT IS ASMR?

5 WHICH SPOOKY TV SERIES INSPIRED A TIKTOK DANCE, BEST PERFORMED IN A BLACK DRESS WITH EYELINER?

ANSWERS ON p76!

74

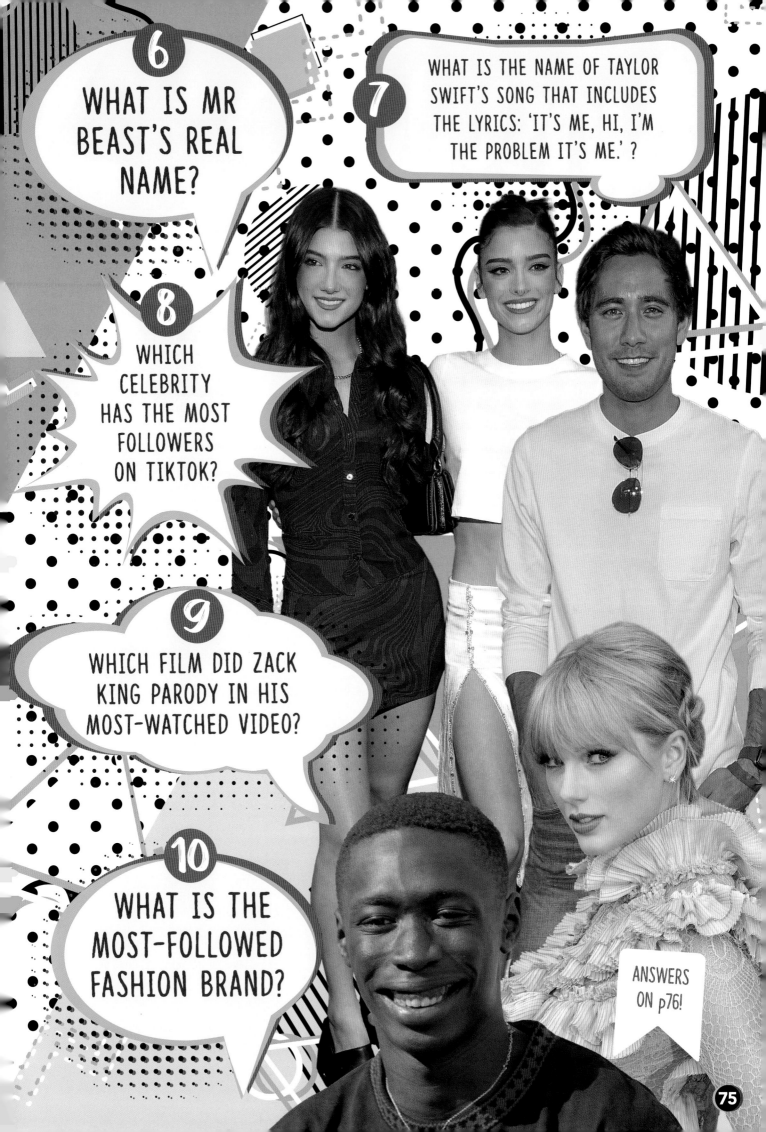

6 WHAT IS MR BEAST'S REAL NAME?

7 WHAT IS THE NAME OF TAYLOR SWIFT'S SONG THAT INCLUDES THE LYRICS: 'IT'S ME, HI, I'M THE PROBLEM IT'S ME.' ?

8 WHICH CELEBRITY HAS THE MOST FOLLOWERS ON TIKTOK?

9 WHICH FILM DID ZACK KING PARODY IN HIS MOST-WATCHED VIDEO?

10 WHAT IS THE MOST-FOLLOWED FASHION BRAND?

ANSWERS ON p76!

75

Answers

p24-25

```
      ¹S T O R Y T I M E
   ²L   L
   I   A              ⁴V
³L O W K E Y           I
   K   Y              E
⁵H A S H T A ⁶G        W
   S       L     ⁷T   S
⁸F O L L O W E R S   E
           O         A
           W         
           U         
         ⁹P F ¹⁰P
               O
               S
             ¹¹T R A C K
```

p56

❶ PLUDOA → ⓐ VIDEO
❷ IVDOE → ⓑ LIKES
❸ KLISE → ⓒ UPLOAD
❹ WIEVS → ⓓ TRENDING
❺ TEDI → ⓔ TUTORIAL
❻ TGENDNRI → ⓕ EDIT
❼ ADCEN → ⓖ STORYTIME
❽ ATORTLU → ⓗ VIEWS
❾ OSYMTERTI → ⓘ DANCE

p57

1. TRUE
2. FALSE - IT CAME SECOND TO INSTAGRAM!
3. TRUE
4. TRUE
5. FALSE - IT'S ACTUALLY AROUND 1.5 HOURS

p60

1 ADDISON RAE

2 MR BEAST

3 MEGHAN TRAINOR

4 TAYLOR SWIFT

5 WILL SMITH

6 ABBY ROBERTS

p69

FOLLOWER - SOMEONE WHO LIKES YOUR ACCOUNT.

FIRE - DESCRIBES SOMETHING THAT YOU THINK IS REALLY GOOD!

NO CAP - TO TELL THE TRUTH.

DEAD - TO FIND SOMETHING INCREDIBLY FUNNY.

PUSHING P - STAYING TRUE TO YOURSELF.

RENT FREE - SOMETHING THAT YOU CAN'T GET OUT OF YOUR HEAD.

SLAY - SOMETHING THAT HAS BEEN DONE WELL, OR LOOKS AMAZING.

TEA - ANOTHER WORD FOR GOSSIP.

STAN - TO WORSHIP SOMETHING OR SOMEONE OBSESSIVELY.

p74

1 DIXIE. 2 IN REAL LIFE. 3 ITALY. 4 A TINGLY FEELING WHEN LISTENING TO SOMETHING. 5 WEDNESDAY. 6 JIMMY. 7 ANTIHERO. 8 WILL SMITH. 9 HARRY POTTER. 10 LOUIS VUITTON.

Picture Credits